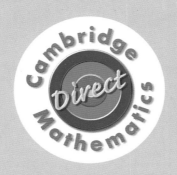

Numbers and
the Number System

4

CAMBRIDGE
UNIVERSITY PRESS

PUBLISHED BY THE PRESS SYNDICATE OF THE UNIVERSITY OF CAMBRIDGE
The Pitt Building, Trumpington Street, Cambridge, United Kingdom

CAMBRIDGE UNIVERSITY PRESS
The Edinburgh Building, Cambridge CB2 2RU, UK
40 West 20th Street, New York, NY 10011–4211, USA
10 Stamford Road, Oakleigh, VIC 3166, Australia
Ruiz de Alarcón 13, 28014 Madrid, Spain
Dock House, The Waterfront, Cape Town 8001, South Africa

http://www.cambridge.org

First published 2000

Printed in the United Kingdom at the University Press, Cambridge

Typefaces Frutiger, Helvetica, Minion, Swift *System* QuarkXPress 4.03®

A catalogue record for this book is available from the British Library

ISBN 0 521 78467 0 paperback

Text illustration by Adam Stower

General editors for Cambridge Mathematics Direct
Sandy Cowling, Jane Crowden, Andrew King, Jeanette Mumford

Writing team for *Numbers and the Number System 4*
Jane Crowden, Jeanette Mumford, Mary Nathan, Fay Turner

The writers and publishers would like to thank the many schools and individuals
who trialled lessons for Cambridge Mathematics Direct.

Abbreviations and symbols
IP Interactive picture
CM Copymaster
A is practice work
B develops ideas
C is extension work
★ if needed, helps with work in A
A red margin indicates that children work with the teacher.
A green margin indicates that children work independently.

Contents

Fractions (F): Fractions and decimals

Introducing thousands

Key idea	10 hundreds are the same as 1 thousand.

Flight facts

Concorde's fuel load is 2830 gallons.

A Jumbo Jet needs a runway of 3400 metres.

The world record distance for a glider is 1460 km.

The world's fastest aeroplane reached a speed of 7254 km per hour.

In 1927 Lindbergh flew solo from New York to Paris, a distance of 5796 km.

A1 Write the value of

a the 2 in 2830

b the 4 in 3400

c the 6 in 1460

d the 2 in 7254

A2 Write each number from 'Flight facts' in words.

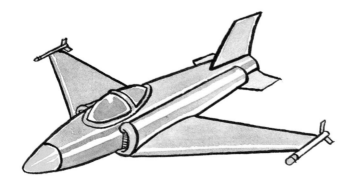

A3

a. $6437 = $  $ + 400 + 30 + 7$

b. $2185 = 2000 + $ ___ $ + 80 + 5$

c. $9279 = 9000 + 200 + $ ___ $ + 9$

d. $3513 = $ ___ $ + 500 + 10 + $ ___

B1

a. Use the digits 2, 4, 6 and 8 to make 4-digit numbers.

There are 24 ways altogether!

Find at least 8.

b. Tick the numbers where the 4 has a value of 400.

c. Cross out the numbers where the 8 has a value of 80 and the 6 has a value of 6000.

C1

You need a set of 0–9 digit cards.

- Place the cards face down.

- Take any 5 cards.

- Write, in numerals and in words, the biggest and the smallest 5-digit numbers you can make from the cards.

Repeat using different cards.

Key idea	10 hundreds are the same as 1 thousand.

Changing thousands

Key idea	When we add or subtract 1 thousand to or from a 4-digit number, the digit in the thousands column changes.

A1 Write the new height for each pilot.

Pilot: Blue Baron	
current height	add 100 more
827	a
959	d
1050	g

Pilot: Mad Max	
current height	drop 10 less
726	b
2036	e
3765	h

Pilot: Red Alert	
current height	add 1000 more
600	c
7070	f
5413	i

A2 Copy and complete this table.

altitude (height)	add 1	add 10	add 100	add 1000
146	147	157		
839				
3025				
4966				
7890				

A3 Find a way to check your answers to A2.
Write down your check for each answer.

How much did you add altogether?

B1 Do CM 1.

B2 'Loop the loop' 4 more times.
Draw your own loops and choose 4-digit numbers.

PV1.3 Comparing numbers and measurements

Key idea	< means 'is less than' and > means 'is greater than'.

A1 | Blue Baron's cockpit

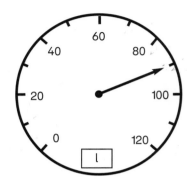 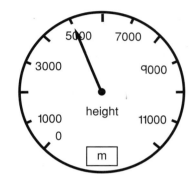 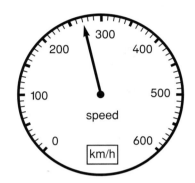

Red Alert's cockpit

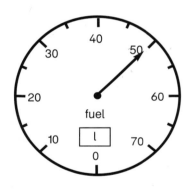 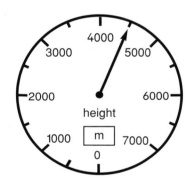 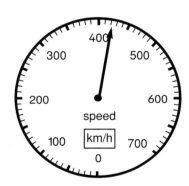

Copy and complete these charts.

a

Blue Baron	reading
fuel	l
height	m
speed	km/h

b

Red Alert	reading
fuel	l
height	m
speed	km/h

Count the small divisions on the dial carefully.

B1

a Which plane has less fuel? _____ because ☐ < ☐

b How many litres less? _____ because ☐ − ☐ = ☐

c Which pilot is flying higher? _____ because ☐ > ☐

d How many metres higher? _____ because ☐ − ☐ = ☐

e What is the difference in speed between the planes?

C1

Four card trick with a difference

Work in pairs.

Use 2 sets of 0–9 cards.

Copy these number sentences.

a ☐ > ☐ > ☐

b ☐ < ☐ < ☐

c ☐ > ☐ > ☐

d ☐ < ☐ < ☐

• Shuffle all the cards and deal 4 each.

• Both make a 4-digit number with your cards.

• Decide together where to place the two numbers in the first number sentence.

• Make up a 4-digit number for the third box to complete the sentence so that it is true.

Do the same to complete all the number sentences.

Key idea	< means 'is less than' and > means 'is greater than'.

Ordering 4-digit numbers

Key idea	To compare numbers with the same number of digits, start at the left and find the first column with different digits. The larger number has the larger digit.

A1 Copy and complete this number line.

A2 Put these numbers in order, smallest first.

A3 For each number line write five 4-digit numbers:

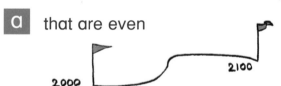

a that are even

2000   2100

b that are odd

5400   5500

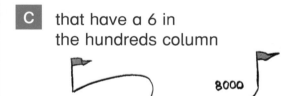

c that have a 6 in the hundreds column

7000   8000

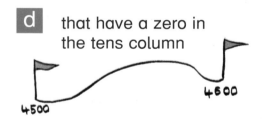

d that have a zero in the tens column

4500   4500

B1 Do CM 4 with a friend.

C1 Palindromes are numbers that read the same backwards as forwards.

Here are some palindromic 4-digit numbers.

There are 90 palindromic 4-digit numbers between 1000 and 10 000.

True or false?

Investigate.

Look for a pattern.

CM 4

Multiplying by 10

| **Key idea** | To multiply a number by 10, move the digits one place to the left. |

A1

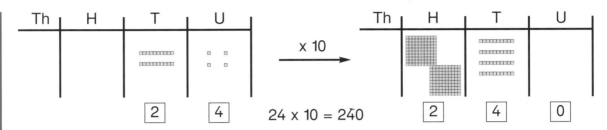

Th	H	T	U		Th	H	T	U

x 10 →

2 4   24 × 10 = 240   2 4 0

Multiply the value on each board by 10.

Write your answers as multiplication sentences.

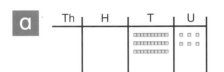
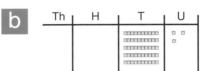
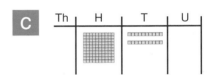

A2

a 15 × 10 = ☐

39 × 10 = ☐

84 × 10 = ☐

b ☐ × 10 = 90

☐ × 10 = 180

☐ × 10 = 270

c 170 × 10 = ☐

☐ × 10 = 2600

420 × ☐ = 4200

B1 Copy and complete these patterns.

a 5 × 10 = ☐

50 × 10 = ☐

500 × 10 = ☐

b 37 × 10 = ☐

370 × 10 = ☐

3700 × 10 = ☐

c ☐ × 10 = 640

640 × 10 = ☐

☐ × 10 = 64000

d Make up 2 patterns of your own.
Try ×100 in one of them.

B2

a Make 6 different 3-digit numbers with these digits.
Use each digit once only in each number.

2 5 7

b Multiply each 3-digit number by 10.

c Order your answers to **b** , starting with the smallest 4-digit number.

PV2.3 Dividing by 10

Key idea	To divide a number by 10, move the digits one place to the right.

A1 Copy and complete the sentences.

a

b

90 daffodils make ☐ bunches.
☐ daffodils in 6 bunches.

☐ roses make 10 bunches.
110 roses in ☐ bunches.

c

d

500 petunias make ☐ trays.
☐ petunias in 70 trays.

300 crocus make ☐ boxes.
☐ crocus in 10 boxes.

A2 **a** Design your own magic maths machine to divide by 10.

b Test your machine by feeding in 7 numbers.

In	Out

B1 Copy and complete.

a 1 flower pot costs £3

10 ⟶ £☐

100 ⟶ £☐

☐ ⟶ £15 000

b 1 house plant costs £12

☐ ⟶ £120

☐ ⟶ £1200

1000 ⟶ £☐

c 100 m of fencing costs £2000   **d** 100 kg of gravel costs £170

10 m   ⟶ £ ☐   10 kg   ⟶ £ ☐

1 m   ⟶ £ ☐   1 kg   ⟶ £ ☐

B2 Find out which numbers
this machine is working on today.

In	Out
40	
	7
100	
900	
	50
8000	
	900

C1 Investigate what happens when these 2 machines are linked.

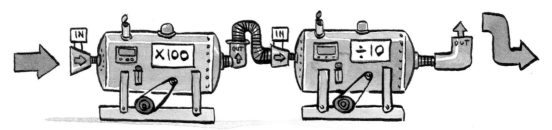

a Feed in 1-digit numbers.
Record in a table.

b Feed in 2-digit numbers.
Record in a table.

Key idea	To divide a number by 10, move the digits one place to the right.

Matching examples

Key idea	When we multiply a number by 100, every digit moves 2 places to the left.

A1 Copy and complete.

a 7 cm × 10 = 70 cm   **b** 70 cm × 10 = 700 cm   **c** 7 cm × 100 = ☐

12 cm × 10 = ☐   120 cm × 10 = ☐   12 cm × 100 = ☐

25 cm × 10 = ☐   250 cm × 10 = ☐   25 cm × 100 = ☐

A2

a 4p × 10 = ☐ p   **b** 40p × 10 = ☐ p

10p × 10 = ☐ p   100p × 10 = ☐ p or £ ☐

80p × 10 = ☐ p or £ ☐   £8 × 10 = £ ☐

c 4p × 100 = ☐ p or £ ☐

10p × 100 = ☐ p or £ ☐

80p × 100 = ☐ p or £ ☐

8 × 100 = 800 Erasers

80 × 10 = 800 Erasers

B1 Miss Gibbons wrote:

8 × 100 = 800 erasers

80 × 10 = 800 erasers

a 6 × 100 = ☐ pens

60 × 10 = ☐ pens

b ☐ × 100 = 1500 jotters

150 × 10 = ☐ jotters

c ☐ × 100 = 3600 glue sticks

☐ × 10 = 3600 glue sticks

B2 **a** Coloured pencils come in packs of 24.
There are 10 packs in a box and 10 boxes.
How many pencils altogether?

b Paint brushes cost £30 for 10.
How much do 100 paint brushes cost?

c 100 paper stars cost £2.
How much do 10 stars cost?
How much does 1 star cost?

C1 Write stock cupboard stories for these answers.

Use all you know about multiplying and dividing by 10 or 100.

| Key idea | When we multiply a number by 100, every digit moves 2 places to the left. |

PV3.1 Using negative numbers

Key idea | The numbers to the right of zero on a number line are positive and the numbers to the left of zero are negative.

A1 Do CM 7.

B1 The seagull is resting on the water, level with step 0.

Write the step number it will face when the tide level

a rises up 2

b rises up 4

c drops down 3

d drops down 5

CM 7

B2 The tide is out. You can see all the steps.

Where does the seagull finish after these hops?

Copy and complete the table.

Start on step	Hop	Finish on step
+2	down 2	
−1	up 3	
+4	down 6	
−3	up 3	
+5	down 10	
−6	up 5	

C1 The seagull hops up 6 steps.
Write down the possible pairs of step numbers at different tide levels in a number sentence.

For example

Start on step	Hop		Finish on step
−1	up 6		5
−1	+ 6	=	5

C2 This time the seagull hops down 3.
Investigate possible number sentences.

Key idea	The numbers to the right of zero on a number line are positive and the numbers to the left of zero are negative.

Ordering on a number line

Key idea	The set of integers has positive and negative numbers and zero.

A1 Find the missing integers on this number line.

A2 Write 2 integers that lie between:

a −2 and 3   b 0 and 5   c −4 and 1   d −12 and −8

B1 a Play the game on CM 8 with a partner.

b Play again.

Keep count of how many moves it takes to win.

Record some of your moves.

World temperatures on 12 December

Athens 18°C
Brussels -2°C
Calgary -12°C
Delhi 23°C
London 6°C
Moscow -9°C
Paris 0°C
Toronto -4°C

B2 Write these temperatures in order, lowest first.

B3 Which of these cities

a is the coldest?

b is the warmest?

c are above 0 °C?

d are below 0 °C?

C1 Name the city that is

a 2 degrees warmer than Brussels

b 5 degrees colder than Toronto

c 12 degrees cooler than Athens

d 32 degrees warmer than Moscow

C2 Find some temperatures in a newspaper.

Make up your own problems as in C1.

| Key idea | The set of integers has positive and negative numbers and zero. |

PV3.3 Reading scales

Key idea	Different scales are used on different instruments.

B1 Write down the lengths **in metres** that the arrows point to.

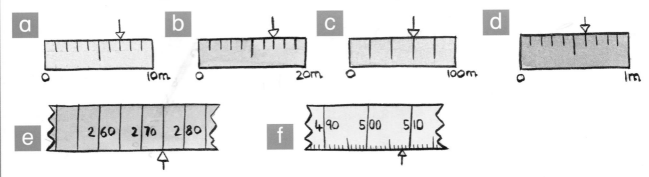

a   0   10m

b   0   20m

c   0   100m

d   0   1m

e   2 60   2 70   2 80

f   4 90   5 00   5 10

B2 Write the amounts in these measuring cylinders.

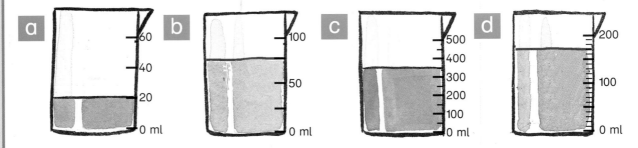

a   60 40 20 0 ml

b   100 50 0 ml

c   500 400 300 200 100 0 ml

d   200 100 0 ml

B3 Write the weights shown on these scales.

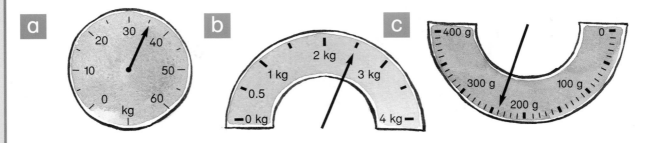

a   0 10 20 30 40 50 60 kg

b   0 kg 0.5 1 kg 2 kg 3 kg 4 kg

c   400 g 300 g 200 g 100 g 0

B4 Write the temperatures shown on these thermometers.

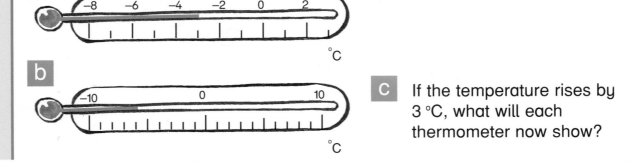

a   −8 −6 −4 −2 0 2 °C

b   −10 0 10 °C

c   If the temperature rises by 3 °C, what will each thermometer now show?

Collections and numbers

Key idea	Sometimes it is more useful to estimate than to count exactly.

A1

a Estimate how many bubbles the fish has made.

b How did you make your estimate?

A2 This picture is the prize for the competition.

a Estimate how many spots are on the fish.

b How did you make your estimate?

A3 Draw an estimating puzzle for a friend.
Group things to make it easier.

B1 Look at the boxes of shells at the bottom of IP 4.

There are 160 shells in the middle box.

a About how many shells are in the box on the left?

b Roughly how many shells are in the box on the right?

c Compare the contents of the boxes and write a sentence about each pair.

B2 Mr Da Silva buys boxes of 100 shells.

Draw 3 boxes that are not full.

Write 3 sentences comparing the numbers of shells in pairs of boxes.

C1 Miss Stefanski wants to give a shell to each child in the juniors.

There are 220 children.

Look at the boxes on IP 4.

a Are there enough shells for each child to have one?

b How many children could have a shell?

C2 Each small tin of fish food holds 100 drops.

Each giant tin of fish food holds 250 drops.

Each fish eats 1 drop a day.

a Estimate how many small tins of fish food are needed to feed all the fish in the tanks on IP 4 each day.

b Estimate how many giant tins of fish food are needed to feed all the fish in the tanks on IP 4 each day.

| **Key idea** | Sometimes it is more useful to estimate than to count exactly. |

Using number lines to round

| Key idea | We can estimate the position of numbers on a number line. This can help us when we round the numbers. |

A1 To the nearest 10 what do these numbers round to?

a 672   b 859   c 314

d 491   e 545   f 612

A2 To the nearest 10 what do these numbers round to?

a 295   b 808   c 697

d 692   e 702   f 391

A3 Look at these number trios.
To the nearest 10, 2 of the numbers round to the same number.
In your book, write the odd one out and the number it rounds to.

a 231, 238, 241

b 649, 653, 656

c 711, 701, 714

C1
a Choose a 3-digit multiple of 10.

b Write down all the numbers that round to it, to the nearest 10.

c What is the difference between the smallest and the largest numbers?

C2 Repeat C1 for other numbers.

What do you notice?

Why is this?

PV4.3 Rounding to 10, 100

Key idea	We can round numbers to the nearest 10 or 100.

B1

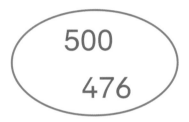

a Find ten numbers that round to the nearest 10 to 250.

b Round each number to the nearest 100.

c What do you notice about your answers to b ?

B2 Repeat B1 for 450 and 750.

B3 Find 20 numbers that round to the nearest 100 to 500.

> 500
>
> 476

C1 When we round to the nearest 100,

a what is the smallest whole number that rounds to 400?

b what is the largest whole number that rounds to 400?

c what is the difference between them?

C2 Choose two more 3-digit multiples of 100 and repeat C1.

C3 Karl finds numbers that round to 3000 to the nearest 1000.

What do you think the difference will be between the smallest and the largest whole numbers?

PV4.4 Approximating

A1 At the aquarium, they are putting pebbles in the tanks.

About how many are there in each tank?

a 341 + 79   b 657 + 234

c 297 + 701   d 482 + 403

Write out the rough calculation.

A2 Which of these is the best approximation for 361 + 486?

a 370 + 480   b 360 + 460   c 400 + 500

d 360 + 490   e 360 + 500

Mr Da Silva needs a new ticket machine.

The table shows how many visitors he had last week.

	Monday	Tuesday	Wednesday	Thursday	Friday
Number of visitors in morning	84	98	104	106	153
Number of visitors in afternoon	129	113	138	157	206

B1 Roughly, how many tickets does the machine have to produce

a on Monday?　　b on Tuesday?　　c on Wednesday?

d on Thursday?　　e on Friday?　　f for a week?

B2 How many visitors actually came to the aquarium on

a on Monday?　　b on Tuesday?

B3 How accurate were your estimates for Monday and Friday?

C1 Make up 3 sums that approximate to

a 800 + 500 (numbers have been rounded to the nearest 10)

b 600 + 300 (numbers have been rounded to the nearest 100)

c 4200 + 3700 (numbers have been rounded to the nearest 100)

C2 Look at IP 4.

Make up 5 sums for the 2 little fish tanks for the rest of the class to solve.

Key idea	We can estimate calculations by approximating.

1s, 10s, 100s and 1000s

Key idea	In a sequence of numbers, look for what is changing and what is staying the same.

Count in 1s, 10s, 100s or 1000s.

A1 Write the number that is:

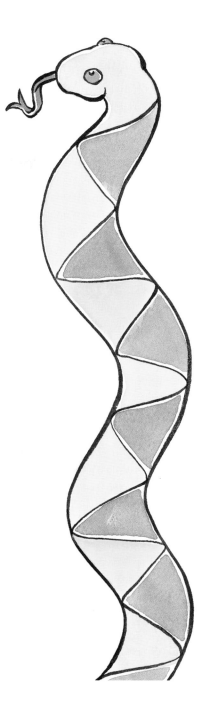

a | 7 more than

500
130
206
477

b | 7 less than

500
130
206
477

c | 70 more than

500
130
206
477

d | 70 less than

500
130
206
477

A2 Write the next 3 numbers in these sequences.

a 500, 510, 520, ☐, ☐, ☐

b 650, 750, 850, ☐, ☐, ☐

c 2240, 2340, 2440, ☐, ☐, ☐

B1 Choose a starting number and a rule to make 8 sequences of 5 numbers.

Starting numbers
406   892
5300   7060

Rules
• Count on in 100s
• Count back in 1000s
• Count on in 1000s
• Count back in 100s
• Count on in 10s

Example

Starting number: 406   Rule: Count on in 10s

406, 416, 426, 436, 446

Think carefully about choosing a good rule for your starting number.

C1 Copy and complete.

start   finish

a   416   +500   ☐   +☐   1916

b   380   +600   ☐   +☐   2980

c   725   +700   ☐   +☐   5425

C2 Make up some more of your own.
Ask a friend to solve them.

| Key idea | In a sequence of numbers, look for what is changing and what is staying the same. |

N1.2 Odds and evens 1

A1

a Copy this table.

Write these numbers in the correct column:

6, 29, 54, 78, 105, 310, 447, 863

odd	even

b Complete this sentence.

The last digit of an odd number is ☐ or ☐ or ☐ or ☐ or ☐

B1

a Choose 2 numbers from the ski hats.

Add them together like this. 5 + 13 = 18

Find 6 different totals.

b Complete this sentence.

When we add 2 odd numbers the answer is _____.

B2

a Make 6 subtraction sentences with these numbers.

b Complete this sentence.

The difference between a pair of odd numbers is _____.

C1 Do CM 15, question 2.

Odds and evens 2

| **Key idea** | We can match examples to a statement to see if it may be true. |

A1 | Do CM 16.

B1 | **Triple odds**

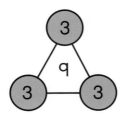

Look at this triangle.
The same odd number is used for the 3 circles.
The triple total is 3 + 3 + 3 = 9

a Find these triple totals.

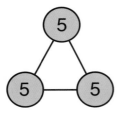 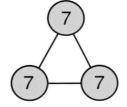 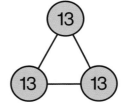

b Find the missing odd numbers to make these triple totals.

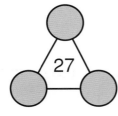 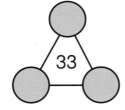 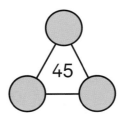

B2

a Find 3 numbers to make these odd trio totals.

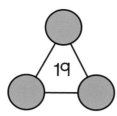 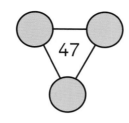 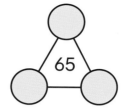

b Are all your numbers odd?

c Choose 2 odd totals and make triangles using odd and even numbers.

C1

Any odd number is double a number, add 1

a Investigate for these numbers.

$$45 = 2 \times 22 + 1$$

$$51 = 2 \times \square + 1$$

$$69 =$$

$$87 =$$

$$93 =$$

b Use the ace to 9 cards from a set of playing cards.

Red cards are tens, black cards are units.

Make 6 more odd numbers with the cards to test the statement.

Record your findings.

| **Key idea** | We can match examples to a statement to see if it may be true. |

N1.4 Fours

A1 Copy and continue these sequences.

a 0, 2, 4, 6, . . . to 20

b 0, 4, 8, 12, . . . to 20

c 40, 38, 36, 34, . . . to 20

d 40, 36, 32, . . . to 20

B1

These numbers were fed into the machine. This is what happened.

In ⟶	Divide by 2 ⟶	Divide by 2 ⟶	Out
4	2	1	1
6	3	–	–
8	4	2	2
12	6	3	3
14	7	–	–
16	8	4	4
17	–	–	–
18	9	–	–

Check the entries in the table.

a The machine gives an OUT answer for some numbers. Which ones?

They are _____ of 4 and are _____ by 4.

b Feed these numbers into the machine. | 20 | 22 | 25 | 28 | 32 | 37 |

Which ones are divisible by 4?

B2 Copy and complete the test report.

Divisible by 4 test
A number has to:
• be an _____ number
• divide exactly by 2 and
  divide exactly by _____ again.

N1.5 Threes

Key idea	If the sum of the digits of a number is divisible by 3, so is the number.

A1 Do CM 19.

A2 **Divisible by 3?**

Use the trick to work out
which numbers are divisible by 3.

Magic trick
$18 : 1 + 8 = 9$
so 18 is divisible by 3

| a | 24 | b | 29 | c | 36 | d | 41 | e | 45 |

B1 Sort the snowboards.

Copy this diagram.

	divisible by 3	not divisible by 3
odd		
even	12	

Write each snowboard number in the correct place.

B2   What if . . . you had a 3-digit number?

Investigate 102. How can you check that the 'trick' works?

C1   Use these digits to make
10 different 3-digit numbers
that are divisible by 3.

What if . . . you
changed 0 to 2?

C2   What if . . . you made 4-digit numbers?

How can you check that the 'trick' works?

| **Key idea** | If the sum of the digits of a number is divisible by 3, so is the number. |

N2.1 2-, 3-, 4- and 5-steps

Key idea	We can predict the next numbers in a sequence by looking at patterns in the numbers.

A1 For each number sequence

- find the next 4 numbers

- write about the pattern

Use a 1–100 square if you need to.

a
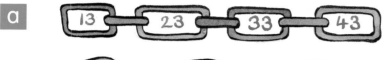
13 23 33 43

b

32 37 42 47

c

107 105 103 101

d

87 91 95 99

A2 Predict the 10th number for each sequence in A1.

B1 For each number sequence

- find the next 3 numbers

- write about the pattern

a

3652 3552 3452 3352

b

218 213 208 203

c

54 57 60 63

B2 Predict the 10th number for each sequence in B1.

B3

Look again at this number sequence.

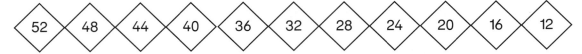

Use 10 × 3 = 30

What is the 10th number?

What is the 20th number?

What is the 30th number?

What is the 100th number?

C1

Look at these sequences.

They both have steps of 4.

a

| | 35 | | 43 | | 51 | | 59 | | 67 | | 75 |
| 31 | | 39 | | 47 | | 55 | | 63 | | 71 | |

b

52 48 44 40 36 32 28 24 20 16 12

For each sequence

• write the rule

• record the units digits in a circle pattern

• investigate this statement:

> For steps of 4, starting with an even number gives a circle pattern of even digits and starting with an odd number gives a circle pattern of odd digits.

C2

What if . . . you make sequences with steps of 2 or 3 or 5 or 10 or 100?

Investigate the circle patterns and write about them.

Key idea | We can predict the next numbers in a sequence by looking at patterns in the numbers.

N2.3 Multiples

Key idea	We can recognise patterns of multiples on a variety of grids.

B1 Copy these grids.

Continue the patterns of 3s.

1	2	3	4	5	6
7	8	9	10	11	12
13	14	15	16	17	18
19	20	21	22	23	24
25	26	27	28	29	30

1	2	3	4
5	6	7	8
9	10	11	12
13	14	15	16
17	18	19	20

a What patterns do you see?

b What is the same about the patterns?

c What is different about the patterns?

B2 Choose 2 different grids of your own.
Decide how many columns and rows they should have.
Draw them on squared paper and colour in multiples of 5 on each grid.

a Write what you notice about the patterns.

b What is the same and what is different about the 2 patterns?

c Why do you think these patterns are like this?

C1 Investigate multiples of 2, 3, 4, 5 and 10 on different grids.

Each time describe the patterns you make.

Write about the similarities and differences between the patterns on the grids.

Think about the size of the grid and the multiple.
How does grid size change the patterns that are made?

More multiples

| Key idea | 100 is a multiple of 5, 25 and 50. |

B1 You need a long strip of paper and crayons in 3 colours.

Use multiples of 5 to make a number snake.

Go to 200 or more.

a Ring all the multiples of 25 in red.

b Ring all the multiples of 50 in yellow.

c Ring all the multiples of 100 in blue.

B2 Copy and complete these sentences.

a Half way between 2 multiples of 50 is a multiple of ☐ .

b Half way between 2 multiples of ☐ is a multiple of 50.

c Every 5th multiple of 5 is a multiple of ☐ .

d Every ☐ th multiple of 25 is a multiple of 100.

e Every 2nd multiple of 25 is a multiple of ☐ .

f 150 and 200 are both multiples of 50.
Half way between them is ☐ which is a multiple of ☐ .

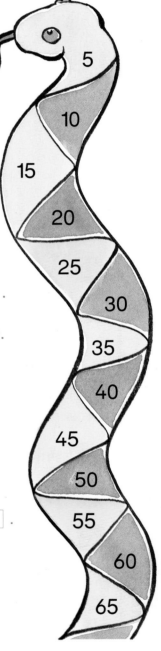

Hari saves a day.

Winston saves   a day.

Emma saves 50p a day.

Shanazara saves £1 a day.

C1 How many days does each child take to save

a £1 **b** £5 **c** £10 **d** £100

C2 **a** Emma wants to save the same amount as Shanazara each day.
How many 50p coins is that?

b Hari wants to save the same amount as Winston each day.
How many 5p coins is that?

c Shanazara has saved £8 in 8 days.
How many days does Winston take to save £8?
Write a sentence to show your working.

C3 Investigate multiples of 75.

Key idea	100 is a multiple of 5, 25 and 50.

Extending counting patterns

| Key idea | Patterns carry on back beyond zero into negative numbers. |

You need 2 friends.

These 3 children started at 3 and recorded sequences.
Peter counted in 2s forwards and backwards.
Kathryn counted in 4s forwards and backwards.
Helena counted in 8s forwards and backwards.

a Do the same from your starting number.

b Look at your sequences.
Talk about these questions.

- Are any of the numbers the same?

- What do you notice about the numbers that are in the 2- and 4- step sequences?

- What do you notice about the numbers that are in the 4- and 8- step sequences?

- What do you notice about the numbers that are in the 2- and 8- step sequences?

- Why are some numbers in all the sequences?

N3.2 Matching examples

B1

Look at the prints in the snow.

a List all the multiples of 4.

b List all the multiples of 3.

B2

a What do you notice about all the multiples of 4?

b Find examples that match your idea.

c What do you notice about all the multiples of 3?

d Find examples that match your idea.

B3

Choose another number.

Investigate its multiples.

Try to make a general statement.

Find examples that match your idea.

C1

  a Write an idea about multiples of 4 and 8.

  b Give supporting evidence.

C2 Do the same for multiples of 3 and 12.

C3 Do the same for multiples of 5 and 15.

Key idea	We can test a general statement by finding examples that match it.

N3 Making decisions and reasoning about numbers

N3.3 Patterns and puzzles

Key idea	We can use what we know about patterns and number operations to solve puzzles.

The first 2 puzzles on this page are a bit easier than the second 2.
Read them all and choose which to do. You can work with a friend.

B1 Try to make all the numbers to 20.
Use the numbers 1, 2, 3 and 4 and
any of the operations +, −, × and ÷.

B2
a What numbers greater than 20 and less than 50 can you make
by finding the sum of 3 consecutive numbers?

$$11 + 12 + 13 = 36$$

b Put your numbers in order.
What do you notice about them?

> 7, 8 and 9 are consecutive numbers. What if I multiply?

C1
a What is 7 × 9?
What is 8 × 8?

b 10, 11 and 12 is another set of consecutive numbers.
What is 10 × 12?
What is 11 × 11?

c Choose some other sets of 3 consecutive numbers.
Multiply the outside numbers. Multiply the inside number by itself.
What do you notice?

d What would happen if…you used groups of 4 consecutive numbers
and multiplied the outside numbers then the inside numbers?

C2
a The consecutive numbers 7 and 8 have a sum of 15 and a product of 56.
Find the consecutive numbers that have these sums and products.

Sum	Product
21	110
13	42
17	72
29	210

b Make up some more of these to challenge your friend.

N3.4 Grid puzzles

| Key idea | We can try out a number and then improve it to make it fit in a missing number sentence. |

C1 Copy and complete the magic square.

3	16	9	22	
	8	21		2
7		13		19
	12	5		6
11		17	10	

C2 Use digit cards 1–9.

Arrange them all to make a magic triangle.

> You need a card at each corner and 2 in between on each side.

C3 Make up some magic squares.

Try a 3 × 3 magic square first, then 4 × 4.

Take out some numbers and swap puzzles with your partner.

N3.5 Growing patterns

Key idea	We can make number patterns by 'growing' shapes.

You need dotty paper.

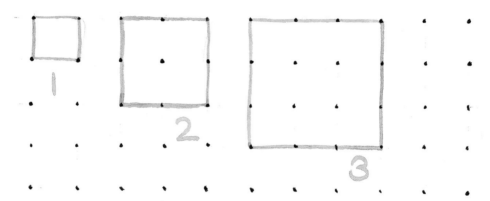

B1   Look at the square 'growing'.

   a   Count the dots on the perimeter (round the edge) of each size of square.

   b   Count the dots inside each square.

   c   Record your results like this.

Square	1	2	3			
Dots on perimeter	4	8				
Dots inside	0	1				

B2   Use dotty paper.

   a   Grow the square some more.
       Carry on counting and recording in your table.

   b   Write about the patterns you see in the rows of the table.

You need squared paper.

Mr Jones wants to make a square pond.

He is going to have one row of square paving all round the pond.

He can't decide how big to make the pond so he tries different sizes on squared paper.

These diagrams show his first two tries.

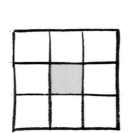 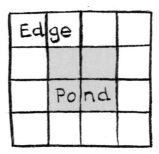

C1   Continue his plans on squared paper.

Find the size of each pond in squares, and the number of slabs to go round it.

Copy and complete the table.

Size of pond in squares	Number of slabs round pond
1	8
4	

C2   a   What pattern can you see in the size of the ponds?

b   What pattern can you see in the number of slabs round the edge of each pond?

c   Can you see see a relationship between the size of pond and the number of slabs round the outside?

Key idea | We can make number patterns by 'growing' shapes.

F1.1 Fractions of shapes

Key idea | $\frac{3}{8}$ means 3 parts out of 8 that make up a whole.

B1 Write the fraction that is shaded.

a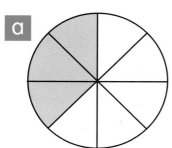

b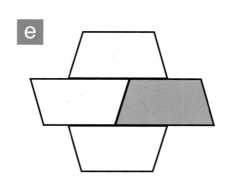

c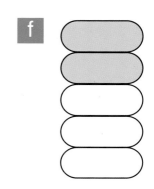

d

e

f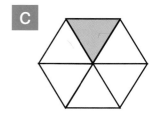

B2 Do CM 26.

C1 Design pairs of labels for the monster's jars.

Make the labels in each pair the same size and shape.

a Divide one into quarters and one into eighths.
Shade $\frac{3}{4}$ of each.

b Divide one into sixths and one into tenths.
Shade $\frac{1}{2}$ of each.

c Shade $\frac{3}{5}$ of each.
Choose your own divisions.

Make sure all the parts of the label are equal.

F1.2 Fractions of numbers 1

Key idea	Divide by 2 to find a half, and by 4 to find a quarter.

A1

a Draw 5 snails. Ring 2 of them.
What fraction of the snails is ringed?

b Draw 8 spiders. Ring 1 of them.
What fraction of the spiders is ringed?

c Draw 3 worms. Ring 2 of them.
What fraction of the worms is ringed?

d Draw 6 beetles. Ring 5 of them.
What fraction of the beetles is ringed?

A2 Find $\frac{1}{2}$ of

a 12   **b** 20   **c** 28   **d** 50   **e** 200

A3 The monster has a recipe for 4.

He wants to make enough for 1.

Find $\frac{1}{4}$ of each item.

MonsterMash
16 worms
20 beetles
32 spiders
40 snails
200 ants

F1 Fractions and division

B1

a The monster had 22 beetles.
He gave half to a friend.
How many did he have left?

b He took 36 spiders out of the jar.
He dropped a quarter of them and they ran away.
How many escaped?

c He needed $\frac{1}{4}$ of his worms to make stew.
There were 44 in the jar.
Write a number sentence to find out how many he used.

B2 There were 28 children in class 4.
Find how many children for each fraction.

a $\frac{1}{2}$ walked to school.

b $\frac{1}{4}$ had a packed lunch.

B3 4 more new children arrived in class 4.
Find the new numbers of children for each fraction.

C1 There were 36 pairs of scissors for class 4.
They lent $\frac{1}{4}$ of them to class 3.
How many were left?

C2

a The monster counted his spiders.
'Oh no!' he shouted. 'There are only 7 left.
$\frac{3}{4}$ of them have escaped.'
How many spiders had he lost?
Explain your working.

b Sort the monster's snails by colour.
$\frac{1}{2}$ are green, $\frac{1}{4}$ are yellow and
the remaining 14 are red.

How many are green?

| **Key idea** | Divide by 2 to find a half, and by 4 to find a quarter. |

F1.3 Fractions of numbers 2

Key idea	We can use division to find a fraction of a number: $\frac{1}{3}$ of 12 = 12 ÷ 3.

A1 Find $\frac{1}{5}$ of

a	20	b	30	c	25	d	50
e	5	f	35	g	45	h	100

A2 Find $\frac{1}{10}$ of

a	40	b	80	c	60	d	100
e	50	f	110	g	70	h	10

A3 3 friends share their picnic equally.

How much do they each have?
Write a number sentence for each item.

B1 Joe walked home from school very slowly. It took him 25 minutes.
Amy went quickly on her bicycle. She got there in one fifth of the time.

How long did she take?

B2 There are 80 children in the school.

One tenth are twins. How many twins?

B3 Make up a fraction problem using one third.

C1 **a** Grace scored 52 points in her computer game.

Ryan only scored three quarters of that.

What was Ryan's score?

Explain how you worked out the answer.

b Megan and James were reading the same book.

James reached page 120.

Megan had read one tenth less.

What page had Megan reached?

Explain how you worked out the answer.

C2 **a** Which would you rather have?

$\frac{1}{3}$ of £39   or $\frac{1}{5}$ of £40

b Make up some 'close' fraction questions to ask your partner.

Key idea	We can use division to find a fraction of a number: $\frac{1}{3}$ of 12 = 12 ÷ 3.

F1.4 Fractions of quantities

Key idea	We can use division to find a fraction of a weight, or a length, or the amount something holds.

You need paper, scissors, string.

A1 Cut 2 strips of paper. Make one 20 cm long. Make the other $\frac{1}{4}$ as long.
Write the length on each strip.

A2 Cut a piece of string 30 cm long. Cut another piece that is $\frac{1}{5}$ of that length.

A3 Draw a 50p coin. Draw another coin that is worth $\frac{1}{5}$ as much.
Write a division sentence.

A4 Look at the 4 jars of coloured water. The fullest, A, holds 1 litre. The one marked B holds 500 ml, C holds 250 ml and D holds 100 ml. One of these is $\frac{1}{4}$ of a litre, one is $\frac{1}{10}$ of a litre and the other is $\frac{1}{2}$ of a litre. Which is which?

B1 On sports day 11 year olds have a 100 m race.
The race for 5 year olds is half that distance.
How far do the 5 year olds run?

B2 How much is $\frac{1}{2}$ of £1?   And $\frac{1}{10}$ of £1?

B3 Tom is making biscuits. He needs $\frac{1}{10}$ kg of sugar. How much is that in grams?

B4 What fraction of 1 metre is 25 cm?   And 20 cm?

B5 5 children bought a large carton of juice to share. It cost 55p.
Each of them paid $\frac{1}{5}$ of the cost. How much was that?

C1 Look at this cake recipe.

100 g butter	260 g flour
120 g sugar	4 eggs
2 teaspoons of lemon juice	

Write the recipe for a cake that is one quarter as big.

C2 **a** Find the number that is $\frac{1}{4}$ of 112.

It is $\frac{1}{3}$ of another number. What number is that?

Explain how you worked it out.

b Write your own puzzle like this.

F1 Fractions and division

F1.5 Investigating fractions

> **Key idea** | The bigger the dividing number in a unit fraction, the smaller the fraction.

B1 Investigate pairs of fractions.

Which fraction in each pair is bigger?

Find 2 examples for each pair.

> Use cubes or counters if it helps.

a $\frac{1}{4}$ and $\frac{1}{5}$ **b** $\frac{1}{5}$ and $\frac{1}{6}$ **c** $\frac{1}{7}$ and $\frac{1}{8}$

Which would you rather have? $\frac{2}{5}$ of my sweets or $\frac{1}{2}$ of my sweets?

C1 Which is bigger?

a $\frac{2}{5}$ or $\frac{1}{2}$ **b** $\frac{2}{7}$ or $\frac{1}{4}$

Investigate.

C2 Make up your own 'Which would you rather have?' questions.

F2.1 Introducing decimal fractions

A1

You need a ruler.

Use the ruler to draw a number line.

Make 11 marks, one every centimetre.

Label one end 0 and the other end 1.

Write the correct decimal fraction at each mark.

A2 Copy and fill in the missing decimal fractions.

B1 Copy and fill in the missing decimal numbers.

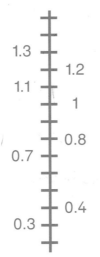

B2 Draw a decimal number line from 0 to 2.

B3 Write how much each child has as a fraction and as a decimal fraction.

  a Jade has 1 slice.

  b Karen has 4 slices.

  c Charlie has 2 slices.

  d Jim has 3 slices.

B4 Write how many mints each child eats as a fraction and as a decimal fraction.

  a Ravi eats 2.

  b Fay eats 4.

  c Ali eats 3.

  d Ellie eats 1.

C1 Greg divides his liquorice string into 10 equal pieces.

On Monday he ate 1 piece.

On Tuesday he ate 3 pieces.

On Wednesday he ate 2 pieces.

On Thursday he ate 4 pieces.

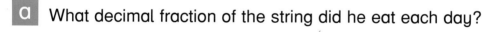

  a What decimal fraction of the string did he eat each day?

  b What fraction did he have left to eat on Friday?

C2 There are 100 pins in the box.
Jane takes 50. Clare takes 20. Arash takes 30.

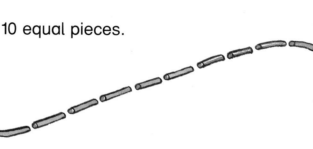

  a What fraction of the whole box does each child have?

  b Write a decimal fraction for each child.

| **Key idea** | One tenth can be written as $\frac{1}{10}$ or as the decimal fraction 0.1 |

Decimal operations

Key idea	The position of a digit in a number gives its value. We can change a tenths digit by adding or subtracting tenths.

Zap the digits

The spaceship can only get rid of the asteroids that are heading for Earth by getting rid of one digit at a time.

Zap as many of the asteroids as you can.

• Make the number on the asteroid with digit cards.

• Use subtraction calculations to zap each digit in turn.

• Record your operations like this:

34.6 − 30 = 4.6

4.6 − 0.6 = 4.0

4.0 − 4 = 0

> You can zap the numbers in any order.

F2.4 Ordering decimals

Help the children in Mrs Turner's class by putting these numbers and measures on the class washing line into order.

★1

a
| 1.8 | 0.3 | 1.6 | 0.5 | 0.9 | 1.1 |

b
| £1.45 | £0.67 | £1.09 | £1.12 | £0.15 |

c
| 1.6 m | 5.0 m | 7.7 m | 0.8 m | 1.4 m |

A1

a
| 1.1 | | 0.4 | | 0.3 | | 1.3 | | 1.8 |
| | 0.5 | | 1.6 | | 0.1 | | 0.9 | | 0.6 |

b
| £1.45 | | £0.67 | | £0.59 | | £1.65 |
| | £1.09 | | £0.23 | | 35p | | £1.12 |

c
| 2.5 m | | 1.4 m | | 5.0 m | | 8.1m |
| | 3.9 m | | 4.1 m | | 0.8 m | | 7.7 m |

Class 4 had a sponsored swimming competition.

B1 These are the times of the first 10 children to swim.

| 4.5 s | 2.9 s | 7.1 s | 8.0 s | 6.9 s |
| 3.4 s | 7.2 s | 5.5 s | 2.8 s | 4.7 s |

Put them in order with the fastest first.

B2 The children raised these amounts of money.

| £6.60 | £6.06 | £3.90 | £8.74 | £2.99 |
| £3.92 | £8.64 | £4.61 | £4.59 | £5.00 |

Put them in order with the most first.

B3 In the gliding competition children stayed afloat for

4.6 m   3.5 m   4.5 m   3.9 m   5.0 m

Put the distances in order, longest first.

C1 You need a page from a catalogue.

a Make a list of all the prices.

b Write them in order from least to most expensive.

| **Key idea** | To put decimals in order, compare the digits in turn, starting from the place with the highest value. |

F2.5 Solving decimal problems

Key idea	We can use what we know about decimals to solve measuring problems.

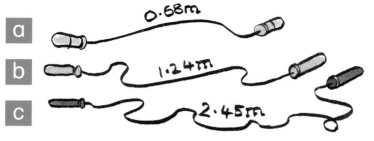

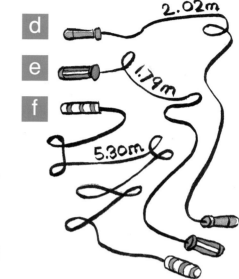

A1 Choose any 2 skipping ropes.
Use any method you like to find their total length.
Record your workings to show your method.
You may cut pieces of string to the two lengths
if you need to.
Write your answers as both centimetres (cm) and
metres (m).

A2 How many more totals of 2 lengths can you find?
Show your workings each time and record your answers as
centimetres (cm) and metres (m).

B1 Choose any 2 skipping ropes.
Use any method you like to find the difference in length between them.
Record your working to show your method.
Write your answer as both centimetres (cm) and metres (m).

B2 Find some other differences between 2 skipping ropes.
Show your workings each time and show your answer
as centimetres (cm) and metres (m).

C1 If you had 4 skipping ropes the length of a how long would they be
if laid end to end?
What about skipping ropes like b ?
Work out some other multiples of the skipping ropes.
Show your workings each time.

C2 Work out what half the length would be for some of the skipping ropes.
Show how you worked them out.

F3.1 Equivalence

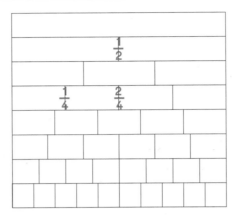

A1 Write the correct fraction on the lines of the fraction wall on CM 34. $\frac{1}{2}$, $\frac{1}{4}$ and $\frac{2}{4}$ are shown here.

A2 Use the wall to help you complete these sentences.

a $\frac{1}{2}$ is the same as $\frac{2}{4}$, $\frac{\square}{6}$, $\frac{4}{\square}$ and $\square$

b $\frac{1}{3}$ is the same as $\square$

c $\frac{1}{5}$ is the same as $\square$

A3 Use the shapes to help you complete the sentences underneath. Write them in your book.

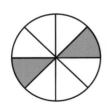 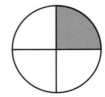

$\frac{2}{8}$ is the same as $\square$

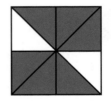 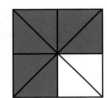

$\frac{6}{8}$ is the same as $\square$

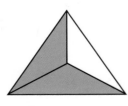 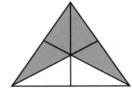

$\frac{2}{3}$ is the same as $\square$

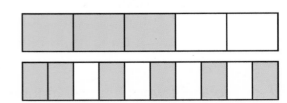

$\frac{3}{5}$ is the same as $\square$

CM 34

1 Write two fractions that describe the pictures below.

The first one has been done for you.

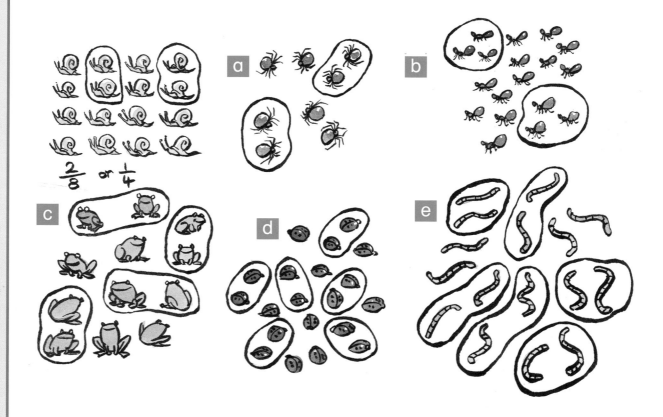

$\frac{2}{8}$ or $\frac{1}{4}$

a

b

c

d

e

C1 Which of these fractions are greater than one half?

$\frac{3}{4}$, $\frac{1}{3}$, $\frac{5}{8}$, $\frac{2}{3}$, $\frac{3}{10}$, $\frac{3}{6}$, $\frac{5}{6}$, $\frac{3}{8}$

C2 You need CM 34.

a Extend the fraction wall to include $\frac{1}{12}$s.

Try $\frac{1}{15}$s as well.

b Find fractions that are the same as

$\frac{3}{12}$, $\frac{4}{12}$, $\frac{9}{12}$, $\frac{6}{15}$, $\frac{12}{15}$

Key idea	We can write the same fraction in different ways. $\frac{1}{2} = \frac{2}{4} = \frac{3}{6} = \frac{4}{8} =$

F3.2 Ordering familiar fractions

Key idea	A mixed number is made up of a whole number and a fraction.

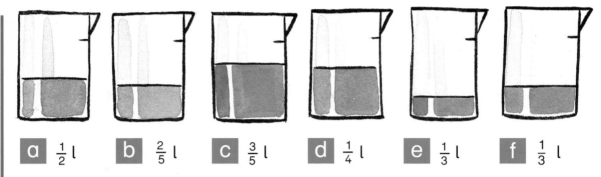

| a $\frac{1}{2}$ l | b $\frac{2}{5}$ l | c $\frac{3}{5}$ l | d $\frac{1}{4}$ l | e $\frac{1}{3}$ l | f $\frac{1}{3}$ l |

A1 Which jug contains the least drink?

A2 Which jug contains the most drink?

A3 Which jugs hold less than $\frac{1}{2}$ l?

B1

a Who is the oldest?

b Who is the youngest?

c Who is older, Fred or Hari?

d Who is younger, Baskar or Eliza?

e Write the children who are 7 in order from the youngest to the oldest.

f Which 2 children are nearest to 9 years old?

g Who is nearest to 8 years old?

Alisha $3\frac{1}{2}$
Baskar $7\frac{1}{4}$
Charlie 2
Dexter $8\frac{3}{4}$
Eliza $7\frac{1}{2}$
Fred $8\frac{1}{4}$
Georgina $9\frac{1}{4}$
Hari $8\frac{1}{2}$
India $3\frac{3}{4}$
Jane $7\frac{1}{3}$

B2 You need CM 34.

The table shows how long it took 5 children to complete a 2 mile sponsored walk.

Who finished a first? b last?

c Who was quicker, Ben or Carrie?

d Did Carries finish before Dan?

Name	Time taken
Annie	$\frac{3}{4}$ h
Ben	$\frac{2}{3}$ h
Carrie	$\frac{7}{10}$ h
Dan	$\frac{5}{8}$ h
Elspeth	$\frac{3}{5}$ h

CM 34

Introducing proportion

> **Key idea** We can compare by using the words 'for every' and 'in every'.

A1

a During term time how many days do you spend at school each week?

In every week I spend ☐ days at school.

b How many days do you spend at school in every 2 weeks?

In every 2 weeks I spend ☐ days at school.

c How many days do you spend at school in every 3 weeks?

In every 3 weeks I spend ☐ days at school.

A2 In every packet of spangles there are 3 lemon sweets.

Answer the following questions beginning your answers with 'In every . . .'.

a How many lemon sweets are there in 2 packets?

b How many lemon sweets are there in 4 packets?

c How many lemon sweets are there in 10 packets?

B1 The children are doing a sponsored walk around the school field.

For every 2 laps of the field they complete they have walked 1 mile.

Begin all your answers 'For every . . .'.

a How far will they have walked for every 4 laps?

b How far will they have walked for every 8 laps?

c How far will they have walked for every 6 laps?

d How far will they have walked for every 10 laps?

F3 Equivalence and ordering

F3.5 Using proportion to solve problems

| Key idea | We can work out proportions to solve problems. |

Write the answers to these problems as sentences.

A1 You need one cup of rice for every 4 people.

How much rice do you need for **a** 8 people? **b** 2 people?

A2 To cook rice you need 3 cups of water for every cup of rice.

How much water for **a** 3 cups of rice? **b** $\frac{1}{2}$ cup of rice?

A3 Mrs Pearce put 6 cups of water in her rice.

a How many cups of rice did she use?

b How many people was she cooking for?

B1 For every £5 that Jayne saves, her grandfather says he will give her £1.

a How much will he give her when she has saved £20?

b How much must she save before he gives her £10?

c How much will he give her when she has saved £35?

d By Christmas Jayne had saved £100 herself.
How much was this with the money from her grandfather?

C1 Find a recipe in a cookery book that you would like to make.

a Work out the ingredients for twice as many people as suggested or half as many people as suggested.

b What ingredients would you need if you cooked it for the whole class?